CITY BY THE BAY

CITY BY THE BAY

SAN FRANCISCO IN ART AND LITERATURE

Edited by Alexandra Chappell

SAN FRANCISCO MUSEUM OF MODERN ART

UNIVERSE PUBLISHING

First published in the United States of America in 2002
by the San Francisco Museum of Modern Art and
UNIVERSE PUBLISHING
A Division of Rizzoli International Publications, Inc.
300 Park Avenue South
New York, NY 10010

2002 2003 2004 2005 2006 2007/ 10 9 8 7 6 5 4 3 2 1

Printed in China.

Director of Publications and Graphic Design, SFMOMA: Kara Kirk
Publications Coordinator, SFMOMA: Alexandra Chappell
Publisher, Universe Publishing: Charles Miers
Editor, Universe Publishing: Christopher Steighner
Designer: Toki Design, San Francisco

City by the Bay: San Francisco in Art and Literature is inspired by
New York, New York: The City in Art and Literature, produced by the
Metropolitan Museum of Art, under the direction of Robie Rogge and
William Lach. It is also available from Universe Publishing.

Library of Congress Control Number: 2001099806
ISBN: 0-7893-0675-1

CONTENTS

The Golden Gate Before the Bridge, San Francisco, California, ca. 1932, printed ca. 1972. Ansel Adams.

IT ONLY TAKES A TINY CORNER OF
This great big world to make a place you love.
My home upon the hill
I find I love you still.
I've been away, but now I'm back to tell you:

San Francisco, open your golden gate
You let no stranger wait outside your door.
San Francisco, here is your wandering one
Saying "I'll wander no more."
Other places only make me love you best
Tell me you're the heart of all the golden west.
San Francisco, welcome me home again
I'm coming home to go roaming no more. [1936]

Golden Gate, 1955. Charles Sheeler.
Overleaf: *Untitled,* 1979. Arthur Ollman.

THURSDAY, 2 NOVEMBER.—SEVERAL OF THE SOLDIERS REQUESTED permission to go hunting, since many deer had been seen. Some of them went quite a long way from the camp and reached the top of the hills, so that they did not return until after nightfall. They said that to the north of the bay they had seen an immense arm of the sea or estuary, which extended inland as far as they could see, to the south-east; that they had seen some beautiful plains studded with trees; and that from the columns of smoke they had noticed all over the level country, there was no doubt that the land must be well populated with natives. This ought to confirm us more and more in the opinion that we were at the port of San Francisco, and that this was the estuary of which the pilot Cabrera Bueno spoke; we had seen its entrance between some ravines while descending the slope of the bay. [1769]

Discovery of the Bay of San Francisco by Portolá, 1896. Arthur Mathews.

ON THE LEE SIDE OF THE HEADLAND WHICH MAKES THE SOUTHERN pilaster of the Gate, sits San Francisco, making of the name she borrowed from the bay a new and distinguished thing, as some women do with their husbands' titles. . . .

. . . From the promontory which makes the northern barrier of the Gate, Tamalpias swims out of atmospheric blueness. On its seaward slope, hardly out of reach of the siren's bellowing note, Muir Park preserves the ancient forest, rooted in the litter of a thousand years. And round about the foot of city and mountain the waters of the bay are blue, the hills are bluer. The hills melt down to greenness in the spring, the water runs to liquid emerald, flashing amber; the hills are tawny after rains, the waters tone to the turbid, clayey river-floods; land and sea they pursue one another as lovers through changing moods of colour; they have mists for mystery between revealing suns. [1914]

Marin Hills, over the Golden Gate from Lincoln Park, San Francisco, ca. 1950, printed ca. 1972. Ansel Adams.

IT WAS IN THE WINTER OF 1835–6 THAT THE SHIP *ALERT*, IN THE prosecution of her voyage for hides on the remote and almost unknown coast of California, floated into the vast solitude of the Bay of San Francisco. All around was the stillness of nature. One vessel, a Russian, lay at anchor there, but during our whole stay not a sail came or went. Our trade was with remote missions, which sent hides to us in launches manned by their Indians. Our anchorage was between a small island, called Yerba Buena, and a gravel beach in a little bight or cove of the same name, formed by two small projecting points. Beyond, to the westward of the landing-place, were dreary sand-hills, with little grass to be seen, and few trees, and beyond them higher hills, steep and barren, their sides gullied by the rains. Some five or six miles beyond the landing-place, to the right, was a ruinous presidio, and some three or four miles to the left was the Mission of Dolores, as ruinous as the presidio, almost deserted, with but few Indians attached to it, and but little property in cattle. Over a region far beyond our sight there were no other human habitations, except that an enterprising Yankee, years in advance of his time, had put up, on the rising ground above the landing, a shanty of rough boards, where he carried on a very small retail trade between the hide ships and the Indians. Vast banks of fog, invading us from the North Pacific, drove in through the entrance, and covered the whole bay; and when they disappeared we saw a few well-wooded islands, the sand-hills on the west, the grassy and wooded slopes on the east, and the vast stretch of the bay to the southward, where we were told lay the Missions of Santa Clara and San José, and still longer stretches to the northward and northeastward, where we understood smaller bays spread out, and large rivers poured in their tributes of waters. There were no settlements on these bays or rivers, and the few ranchos →

Yerba Buena, 1847, 1847. Victor Prevost (attrib.)

and missions were remote and widely separated. Not only the neighbourhood of our anchorage, but the entire region of the great bay was a solitude. On the whole coast of California there was not a lighthouse, a beacon, or a buoy; and the charts were made up from old and disconnected surveys by British, Russian, and Mexican voyagers. Birds of prey and passage swooped and dived about us, wild beasts ranged through the oak groves, and as we slowly floated out of the harbour with the tide, herds of deer came to the water's edge, on the northerly side of the entrance, to gaze at the strange spectacle.

On the evening of Saturday, the 13th of August 1859, the superb steamship *Golden Gate*, gay with crowds of passengers, and lighting the sea for miles around with the glare of her signal lights of red, green, and white, and brilliant with lighted saloons and state-rooms, bound up from the Isthmus of Panama, neared the entrance to San Francisco, the great centre of a world-wide commerce. Miles out at sea, on the desolate rocks of the Farallones, gleamed the powerful rays of one of the most costly and effective lighthouses in the world. As we drew in through the Golden Gate, another lighthouse met our eyes, and in the clear moonlight of the unbroken Californian summer we saw, on the right, a large fortification, protecting the narrow entrance, and just before us the little island of Alcatraz confronted us—one entire fortress. We bore round the point towards the old anchoring-ground of the hide ships, and there, covering the sand-hills and the valleys, stretching from the water's edge to the base of the great hills, and from the old presidio to the mission, flickering all over with the lamps of its streets and houses, lay a city of one hundred thousand inhabitants. Clocks tolled the hour of midnight from its steeples, but the city was alive from the salute of our guns, spreading the news that the fortnightly steamer had come, bringing mails and

San Francisco from Goat Island (detail), 1881. Raymond Dabb Yelland.

passengers from the Atlantic world. Clipper ships of the largest size lay at anchor in the stream, or were girt to the wharves; and capacious high-pressure steamers, as large and showy as those of the Hudson or Mississippi, bodies of dazzling light, awaited the delivery of our mails, to take their cruises up the bay, stopping at Benicia and the United States Naval Station, and then up the great tributaries—the Sacramento, San Joaquin, and Feather rivers—to the far inland cities of Sacramento, Stockton, and Marysville. [1869]

IT IS EASY FOR PLEASURE-LOVING PEOPLE TO FIND AMUSEMENT IN
San Francisco. There are the French and American theatres and the
circus; women and good restaurants abound; and the streets swarm
with horses and carriages. For a time there were no public dances.
Shortly before my arrival this defect was remedied by the proprietors of
the California Exchange, who had the happy idea of giving dances in
this large hall where much business is transacted by day and which is
used as a stock-exchange. Now absolutely nothing is lacking, and a
perpetual carnival reigns. [1851]

The Dancers in a City #2, 1972. Joan Brown.

THE VILLAGE OF YERBA BUENA, FOUNDED IN 1769 BY A SPANISH
expedition, had fewer than fifteen hundred inhabitants, but the adven-
turers had begun to flock in with the first news of gold. Within a few
months, that innocent little village awakened with the name San Francisco and a fame that had reached the farthest points of the globe.
More than a true city, it was an enormous camp for men on the move.

Gold fever left no one unaffected: smiths, carpenters, teachers,
doctors, soldiers, fugitives from the law, preachers, bakers, revolution-
aries, and harmless madmen of various stripes who had left family
and possessions behind to traverse half the world in search of
adventure. "They look for gold, and along the way lose their souls,"
Captain Katz had repeated tirelessly in the brief religious services
he imposed every Sunday on the passengers and crew of the *Emilia*,
but no one paid any attention, blinded by dreams of the sudden
riches that would change their lives. For the first time in history, gold
lay scattered on the ground, unclaimed, free, and plentiful, within
the reach of anyone with the will to go after it. Argonauts came from
distant shores: Europeans fleeing wars, plagues, and tyrannies;
Americans, ambitious and short-tempered; blacks pursuing freedom;
Oregonians and Russians dressed in deerskin, like Indians; Mexicans,
Chileans, and Peruvians; Australian bandits; starving Chinese peasants
who were risking their necks by violating the imperial order against
leaving their country. All races flowed together in the muddy alleyways
of San Francisco. [1999]

San Francisco in July, 1849 (detail), 1891. George Henry Burgess.

IN THE FALL OF 1850 WE WERE ALL EXCITEMENT TO HEAR THE result of California's knock at the door of the Union; and as the day approached when the steamer would bring the decision, many eyes were strained toward Telegraph Hill. At length the signal went up— the *Oregon* was outside the heads and would soon be in the harbor. As she neared, another signal indicated that she carried flying colors, implying good news, and presently she appeared in sight to those, who like ourselves overlooked North Beach, gay with streamers and flags of all nations,—the Stars and Stripes most prominent, and, above them, straightened out by the generous wind which seemed to blow a long breath on purpose, floated the longest streamer of all, displaying the words "California Admitted"!

The roar of cannon rolled over the waters, and met answering roars from fort and ships. Everybody was laughing. "Now we were at home again!" cried one. "Yes," was the answer, "and remember, all, we must no more talk of going to 'The States' nor hearing from 'The States.' We are *in* 'The States'!" [1932]

Admission Day, 1909. Willard E. Worden.

W.E.Worden
Photo. S.F.

NO, THE ROAD WAS NOT ENCUMBERED BY CARRIAGES—WE HAD IT all to ourselves. I suppose the reason was, that most people do not like to enjoy themselves too much, and therefore they do not go out to the Cliff House in the cold and the fog, and the dread silence and solitude of four o'clock in the morning. They are right. The impressive solemnity of such a pleasure trip is only equalled by an excursion to Lone Mountain in a hearse. . . .

From the moment we left the stable, almost, the fog was so thick that we could scarcely see fifty yards behind or before, or over-head; and for a while, as we approached the Cliff House, we could not see the horse at all, and were obliged to steer by his ears, which stood up dimly out of the dense white mist that enveloped him. But for those friendly beacons, we must have been cast away and lost.

I have no opinion of a six-mile ride in the clouds; but if I ever have to take another, I want to leave the horse in the stable and go in a balloon. I shall prefer to go in the afternoon, also, when it is warm, so that I may gape, and yawn, and stretch, if I am drowsy, without disar-ranging my horse-blanket and letting in a blast of cold wind.

We could scarcely see the sportive seals out on the rocks, writhing and squirming like exaggerated maggots, and there was nothing sooth-ing in their discordant barking, to a spirit so depressed as mine was.

Harry took a cocktail at the Cliff House, but I scorned such in-effectual stimulus; I yearned for fire, and there was none there; they were about to make one, but the bar-keeper looked altogether too cheerful for me—I could not bear his unnatural happiness in the midst of such a ghastly picture of fog, and damp, and frosty surf, and dreary solitude. I could not bear the sacrilegious presence of a pleasant face at such a time; it was too much like sprightliness at a funeral, and we fled from it down the smooth and vacant beach. [1864]

Studio Portrait in front of Cliff House, 1880s or 1890s. Unknown.

Untitled (detail), 1905, printed 1967. Adolf Dittmer.

WITHIN THE MEMORY OF PERSONS NOT YET OLD, A MARINER
might have steered into these narrows—not yet the Golden Gates—
opened out the surface of the bay—here girt with hills, there lying
broad to the horizon—and beheld a scene as empty of the presence,
as pure from the handiwork, of man, as in the days of our old sea-
commander. . . . Now, a generation later, a great city covers the sand-
hills on the west, a growing town lies along the muddy shallows of the
east; steamboats pant continually between them from before sunrise
till the small hours of the morning; lines of great sea-going ships lie
ranged at anchor; colours fly upon the islands; and from all around the
hum of corporate life, of beaten bells, and steam, and running carriages, goes cheerily abroad in the sunshine. Choose a place on one
of the huge throbbing ferry-boats, and, when you are midway between
the city and the suburb; look around. The air is fresh and salt as if
you were at sea. On the one hand is Oakland, gleaming white among
its gardens. On the other, to seaward, hill after hill is crowded and
crowned with the palaces of San Francisco; its long streets lie in regu-
lar bars of darkness, east and west, across the sparkling picture; a
forest of masts bristles like bulrushes about its feet; nothing remains
of the days of Drake but the faithful trade-wind scattering the smoke,
the fogs that will begin to muster about sundown, and the fine bulk
of Tamalpais looking down on San Francisco, like Arthur's Seat on
Edinburgh. [1883]

copyrighted 1904
by W. E. Worden

Ships on the Bay, Golden Gate, 1904. Willard E. Worden.

THE STREET NEVER FAILED TO INTEREST HIM. IT WAS ONE OF those cross streets peculiar to Western cities, situated in the heart of the residence quarter, but occupied by small tradespeople who lived in the rooms above their shops. There were corner drug stores with huge jars of red, yellow, and green liquids in their windows, very brave and gay; stationers' stores, where illustrated weeklies were tacked upon bulletin boards; barber shops with cigar stands in their vestibules; sad-looking plumbers' offices; cheap restaurants, in whose windows one saw piles of unopened oysters weighted down by cubes of ice, and china pigs and cows knee deep in layers of white beans. At one end of the street McTeague could see the huge power-house of the cable line. Immediately opposite him was a great market; while farther on, over the chimney stacks of the intervening houses, the glass roof of some huge public baths glittered like crystal in the afternoon sun. Underneath him the branch post-office was opening its doors, as was its custom between two and three o'clock on Sunday afternoons. An acrid odor of ink rose upward to him. Occasionally a cable car passed, trundling heavily, with a strident whirring of jostled glass windows. [1899]

Market Scene, Sansome Street, San Francisco, 1872. **William Hahn.**

THE EARTHQUAKE SHOOK DOWN IN SAN FRANCISCO HUNDREDS OF thousands of dollars' worth of walls and chimneys. But the conflagration that followed burned up hundreds of millions of dollars' worth of property. There is no estimating within hundreds of millions the actual damage wrought. Not in history has a modern imperial city been so completely destroyed. San Francisco is gone. Nothing remains of it but memories and a fringe of dwelling-houses on its outskirts. Its industrial section is wiped out. Its business section is wiped out. Its social and residential section is wiped out. The factories and warehouses, the great stores and newspaper buildings, the hotels and the palaces of the nabobs, are all gone. Remains only the fringe of dwelling houses on the outskirts of what was once San Francisco.

Within an hour after the earthquake shock the smoke of San Francisco's burning was a lurid tower visible a hundred miles away. And for three days and nights this lurid tower swayed in the sky, reddening the sun, darkening the day, and filling the land with smoke.

On Wednesday morning at a quarter past five came the earthquake. A minute later the flames were leaping upward. In a dozen different quarters south of Market Street, in the working-class ghetto, and in the factories, fires started. There was no opposing the flames. There was no organization, no communication. All the cunning adjustments of a twentieth century city had been smashed by the earthquake. The streets were humped into ridges and depressions, and piled with the débris of fallen walls. The steel rails were twisted into perpendicular and horizontal angles. The telephone and telegraph systems were disrupted. And the great water-mains had burst. All the shrewd contrivances and safeguards of man had been thrown out of gear by thirty seconds' twitching of the earth-crust. →

Left and previous pages: *Untitled,* from *The San Francisco Earthquake and Fire,* 1906. Arnold Genthe.

41

By Wednesday afternoon, inside of twelve hours, half the heart of the city was gone. At that time I watched the vast conflagration from out on the bay. It was dead calm. Not a flicker of wind stirred. Yet from every side wind was pouring in upon the city. East, west, north, and south, strong winds were blowing upon the doomed city. The heated air rising made an enormous suck. Thus did the fire itself build its own colossal chimney through the atmosphere. Day and night this dead calm continued, and yet, near to the flames, the wind was often half a gale, so mighty was the suck.

Wednesday night saw the destruction of the very heart of the city. Dynamite was lavishly used, and many of San Francisco's proudest structures were crumbled by man himself into ruins, but there was no withstanding the onrush of the flames. Time and again successful stands were made by the fire-fighters, but every time the flames flanked around on either side, or came up from the rear, and turned to defeat the hard-won victory.

An enumeration of the buildings destroyed would be a directory of San Francisco. An enumeration of the buildings undestroyed would be a line and several addresses. An enumeration of the deeds of hero-ism would stock a library and bankrupt the Carnegie medal fund. An enumeration of the dead—will never be made. All vestiges of them were destroyed by the flames. The number of the victims of the earth-quake will never be known. South of Market Street, where the loss of life was particularly heavy, was the first to catch fire.

Remarkable as it may seem, Wednesday night, while the whole city crashed and roared into ruin, was a quiet night. There were no crowds. There was no shouting and yelling. There was no hysteria, no disorder. I passed Wednesday night in the path of the advancing →

Looking up Market Street towards Twin Peaks, 1906. Arnold Genthe.

flames, and in all those terrible hours I saw not one woman who wept, not one man who was excited, not one person who was in the slightest degree panic-stricken.

Before the flames, throughout the night, fled tens of thousands of homeless ones. Some were wrapped in blankets. Others carried bundles of bedding and dear household treasures. Sometimes a whole family was harnessed to a carriage or delivery wagon that was weighted down with their possessions. Baby buggies, toy wagons, and go-carts were used as trucks, while every other person was dragging a trunk. Yet everybody was gracious. The most perfect courtesy obtained. Never, in all of San Francisco's history, were her people so kind and courteous as on this night of terror. [1906]

Left: *Untitled,* from *The San Francisco Earthquake and Fire,* 1906. Arnold Genthe.
Right: *Untitled,* 1906. Arnold Genthe.

IN 1903 MY FATHER WAS BORN IN SAN FRANCISCO, WHERE MY grandmother had come disguised as a man. Or, Chinese women once magical, she gave birth at a distance, she in China, my grandfather and father in San Francisco. She was good at sending. Or the men of those days had the power to have babies. If my grandparents did no such wonders, my father nevertheless turned up in San Francisco an American citizen.

He was also married at a distance. My mother and a few farm women went out into the chicken yard, and said words over a rooster, a fierce rooster, red of comb and feathers; then she went back inside, married, a wife. She laughs telling this wedding story; he doesn't say one way or the other.

When I asked MaMa why she speaks different from BaBa, she says their parents lived across the river from one another. Maybe his village was America, the river an ocean, his accent American. [1977]

A Corner in Chinatown S.F., ca. 1923. P. Douglas Andersen.

THE EIGHT BOYS OF THE WARD FOR SMALL BOYS WERE TAKEN BY streetcar and ferry boat by Blanche Fulton to the Fair in San Francisco. We were supremely well-behaved, not because we enjoyed being well-behaved but because it was part of our agreement with Blanche Fulton. She told us quite plainly that she could manage eight small boys at a World's Fair only if they were well-behaved, and we instantly agreed that we would do only that which she asked us to do, and nothing else. And we didn't break our word. Blanche Fulton took pride in us that whole day. Our clothes were all freshly cleaned and ironed, put on after we had had baths that morning. Every boy presented a picture of a healthy, clean, well-dressed, serious-minded inmate of an orphanage, but of course we didn't think of ourselves in that way at all. The fact is we didn't think of ourselves at all, we thought of the Fair, the wonders ahead. The whole day was to be spent at the Fair, and Miss Fulton, out of her own generous pocket and heart, was going to treat us to a good lunch, and to some of the other refreshments we might see and need. She was a rare old maid. Unpaid volunteer, she achieved more important things on behalf of the kids than any of the other people at the Orphanage. What's more, she liked the kids. She spoke to them by name, and with obvious love, or the disappointment of one whose love has been betrayed.

Four on one side of her, four on the other, we strolled about the Fair. Suddenly from around a magnificent oriental building two camels appeared, followed by four Arabs in colorful costumes. One of them was making strange music on a pipe of some kind. I was so surprised and delighted that the image and sound have stayed with me ever since. We saw an airplane flying very low over the waters of the Golden Gate, and then we saw it quickly rise high and begin to do what was →

The Palace of Fine Arts, 1916. Colin Campbell Cooper.

then called a loop-the-loop. We saw shining, almost imaginary buildings, full of unbelievable works of sculpture, painting, weaving, basketmaking, products of agriculture, and all kinds of mechanical inventions. It was too much of course for one day, but even when it was time to leave we did so with great reluctance, looking back as if we had been in a place that couldn't possibly be real.

We sat at two outdoor tables for a very simple lunch that cost Blanche Fulton twenty-five cents each. And in the late afternoon she bought each of us a Scotch scone for a nickel apiece. I looked at the two women who prepared the hot scones and served them, because I had heard that my mother worked at the Fair selling Scotch scones, but I didn't see her. It was all right, though. I was well, and having the most incredible time I had ever had.

The whole place was all great space, all light, many sounds, including the human voice, much music, and many delicious and unknown but fascinating odors.

We arrived back at the Orphanage in time for a big meat-pie dinner at our own table, and after dinner all of the big boys who had not yet been to the Fair came to ask us about it. [1972]

Right and overleaf: *Untitled,* **from an album of Panama Pacific International Exposition photographs, 1915. Unknown.**

COMING HOME FROM OTHER CITIES AND OTHER PARTS, ONE
crosses the Bay to reach San Francisco and sees first the gray sil-
houette of her hills, shingled with roofs and roofs and roofs; the royal
fringe of masts and spars along her waterfronts; the gray fog circling
and fuming softly over it all, and the gulls flying and crying. The little
boats, plying to and fro, sound their hoarse, sweet notes of warning,
and perhaps the noon whistles and the Angelus bells take up the
sound in a long chord that to some hearts says, "Welcome home!"

Each to his own city. But do you love them as we do, I wonder,
you whose cities are not steep and narrow streeted, scented with the
spices of the Orient and the good tarry smell of ships and fishing,
lulled by the deep rushing of ocean surges on a long beach, and
the lapping of bay water against piers? [1932]

From Nob Hill, n.d. Alfred Bendiner.

THE CABLE-CARS HAVE FOR ALL PRACTICAL PURPOSES MADE SAN
Francisco a dead level. They take no count of rise or fall, but slide
equably on their appointed courses from one end to the other of a six-
mile street. They turn corners almost at right angles; cross other lines,
and, for aught I know, may run up the sides of houses. There is no
visible agency of their flight; but once in a while you shall pass a five-
storied building, humming with machinery that winds up an everlasting
wire-cable, and the initiated will tell you that here is the mechanism.
I gave up asking questions. If it pleases Providence to make a car run
up and down a slit in the ground for many miles, and if for twopence-
halfpenny I can ride in that car, why shall I seek the reasons of the
miracle? [1889]

Left: *Cable Car,* n.d. Max Yavno.
Right: *Untitled,* 1947. Max Yavno.

WHEN I ARRIVED, NOBODY ASKED ME QUESTIONS. THE AUTHORITIES
looked at my papers and stamped me in. I decided to go first to a San
Francisco address given to me by this girl in Peking. The bus put me
down on a wide street with cable cars. This was California Street.
I walked up this hill and then I saw a tall building. This was Old St.
Mary's. Under the church sign, in handwritten Chinese characters,
someone had added: "A Chinese Ceremony to Save Ghosts from
Spiritual Unrest 7 A.M. and 8:30 A.M." I memorized this information
in case the authorities asked me where I worshipped my religion.
And then I saw another sign across the street. It was painted on the
outside of a short building: "Save Today for Tomorrow, at Bank of
America." And I thought to myself, This is where American people
worship. See, even then I was not so dumb! Today that church is the
same size, but where that short bank used to be, now there is a tall
building, fifty stories high, where you and your husband-to-be work
and look down on everybody.

My daughter laughed when I said this. Her mother can make a
good joke. [1989]

Untitled, n.d. Dong Kingman.

"HOW CAN ANYBODY LIVE LIKE THIS?" THE STRANGER MIGHT ASK at that point and Schultz would shrug:

"Oh, they manage. Some live in flophouses, some in third-rate hotels or roominghouses, some in cheap one-room apartments. It all depends. Most of them go up to St. Anthony's Kitchen for a free hot meal at noon. And then there's the Skid Row soup line in the evening, of course. Some are on pension, like the women . . ."

Schultz would stare down the street with piercing blue eyes, wrinkling his nose, and go on: "There are even those who live mostly out of garbage cans . . . and sleep? Don't ask me. If they drink up the flophouse money they've bummed, maybe it's an alley or doorway or under the Bay Bridge ramps—wherever they happen to pass out. After all, it's Skid Row. It's bad down there . . . filthy, horrible! It's almost unbelievable! And yet . . ."

Schultz would pause, a slow smile on his intelligent Prussian face, knowing what always came next. "And yet," he would go on at last, "even on Skid Row there are those who call themselves 'The Happy Ones.' Even down there, you'll find some—more than you'd think—people who somehow haven't lost their sense of humor and their abiding faith in God. [1962]

Five Workers against Concrete Wall, Industrial District, San Francisco, 1933. Dorothea Lange.

WITHIN HALF A DOZEN BLOCKS OF THE CORONET SPADE LEFT THE car and went into the vestibule of a tall brown apartment-building. He pressed three bell-buttons together. The street-door-lock buzzed. He entered, passed the elevator and stairs, went down a long yellow-walled corridor to the rear of the building, found a back door fastened by a Yale lock, and let himself out into a narrow court. The court led to a dark back street, up which Spade walked for two blocks. Then he crossed over to California Street and went to the Coronet. It was not quite half-past nine o'clock.

The eagerness with which Brigid O'Shaughnessy welcomed Spade suggested that she had been not entirely certain of his coming. She had put on a satin gown of the blue shade called Artoise that season, with chalcedony shoulder-straps, and her stockings and slippers were Artoise.

The red and cream sitting-room had been brought to order and livened with flowers in squat pottery vases of black and silver. Three small rough-barked logs burned in the fireplace. Spade watched them burn while she put away his hat and coat.

"Do you bring me good news?" she asked when she came into the room again. Anxiety looked through her smile, and she held her breath.

"We won't have to make anything public that hasn't already been made public."

"The police won't have to know about me?"

"No."

She sighed happily and sat on the walnut settee. Her face relaxed and her body relaxed. She smiled up at him with admiring eyes. "However did you manage it?" she asked more in wonder than in curiosity. →

Nob Hill, San Francisco, 1938, printed ca. 1974. John Gutmann.

"Most things in San Francisco can be bought, or taken."

"And you won't get into trouble? Do sit down." She made room for him on the settee.

"I don't mind a reasonable amount of trouble," he said with not too much complacence.

He stood beside the fireplace and looked at her with eyes that studied, weighed, judged her without pretense that they were not studying, weighing, judging her. She flushed slightly under the frankness of his scrutiny, but she seemed more sure of herself than before, though a becoming shyness had not left her eyes. He stood there until it seemed plain that he meant to ignore her invitation to sit beside her, and then crossed to the settee.

"You aren't," he asked as he sat down, "exactly the sort of person you pretend to be, are you?" [1929]

Yellow Lampshade, 1969, Elmer Bischoff.

ON THURSDAY MORNING FIGHTING ON THE EMBARCADERO BEGAN AS punctually as if the combatants had punched a time clock, stuck their cards in a rack, and turned to. There were no preliminaries this time. They just took up where they left off.

Newspapers announced that the "opening of the port" would be resumed promptly at 8 a.m. Spectators had come early to "get a seat." Teeming thousands covered the hillsides. Enterprising vendors moved about hawking chocolate bars, chewing gum, and cigarets. Since last Tuesday picket lines had swollen to unheard of proportions. Many high school and college boys, unknown to their parents, had put on old clothes and gone down to fight with the union men. Hundreds of workingmen started for work, then changed their minds and went down to the picket lines.

Approximately 800 police were on duty hefting brand new riot sticks, extra long and extra heavy. Others carried sawed-off shotguns and riot guns. The "Martian monsters" were on hand in their gas masks, heavy bags of hand grenades slung about their necks.

At 7 a.m. a string of empty boxcars was sent rattling down the Embarcadero behind a locomotive. Strikers shouted at the scab train crew but made no effort to interfere with it.

Shortly before the 8 a.m. deadline a locomotive shunted two refrigerator cars into the Matson docks. A cry went up from 2,000 pickets assembled nearby.

Still no action. →

San Francisco Strike, 1933. Dorothea Lange.

At 8 a.m. promptly the police went into action. Tear gas bombs were hurled into the picket lines and the police charged with their clubs. Gasping and choking, the strikers were driven back to the alleys off the Embarcadero, or retreated up Rincon Hill.

A couple of blocks away from the point of the first attack, two boxcars standing on a siding burst into flames.

Shots rang out as the police opened fire with revolvers. Flying bricks and bullets crashed windows. Tear gas again sent workers in nearby factory and office buildings swarming to the streets. The whole area was swept by a surf of fighting men. [1949]

Trouble in Frisco, n.d. Fletcher Martin.

"Rumble in Frisco"   Fletcher Martin

TO SAN FRANCISCANS "THE CITY THAT KNOWS HOW" WAS THE BAY, the fog, Sir Francis Drake Hotel, Top o' the Mark, Chinatown, the Sunset District and so on and so forth and so white. To me, a thirteen-year-old Black girl, stalled by the South and Southern Black life style, the city was a state of beauty and a state of freedom. The fog wasn't simply the steamy vapors off the bay caught and penned in by hills, but a soft breath of anonymity that shrouded and cushioned the bashful traveler. I became dauntless and free of fears, intoxicated by the physical fact of San Francisco. Safe in my protecting arrogance, I was certain that no one loved her as impartially as I. I walked around the Mark Hopkins and gazed at the Top o' the Mark, but (maybe sour grapes) was more impressed by the view of Oakland from the hill than by the tiered building or its fur-draped visitors. For weeks, after the city and I came to terms about my belonging, I haunted the points of interest and found them empty and un–San Francisco. The naval officers with their well-dressed wives and clean white babies inhabited another time-space dimension than I. The well-kept old women in chauffeured cars and blond girls in buckskin shoes and cashmere sweaters might have been San Franciscans, but they were at most gilt on the frame of my portrait of the city. [1969]

San Francisco, 1955–66. Robert Frank.

I'VE SEEN MANY CITIES BUILT ABOVE THE SEA. AS DIFFERENT AS Marseilles, Algiers, Lisbon, and Naples are, they all have a common feature: their hills are used as architectural elements. The streets marry their curves; they climb in spirals so artfully that the sea can be glimpsed from almost anyplace. What looks so complicated on a map seems simple and natural in reality. But it's quite the opposite here: San Francisco is a shockingly stubborn abstraction, a geometric delirium. The plan was traced on paper without the architect even glancing at the site. It's a checkerboard pattern of straight lines and right angles, just as in New York or Buffalo. The hills, those very material obstructions, are simply denied; the streets scale up them and hurry down without deviating from their rigid design. As a result, you hardly ever see the ocean. Enclosed between successive barriers that cut off the horizon, the streets have a provincial calm; they are paved with red bricks that evoke the fresh tiling of Dutch kitchens and are lined with white houses three or four stories high. San Francisco does not have the warm, cosmopolitan colors of Barcelona or Marseilles. The memory of the gold miners, their camps, and their brawls seems far away. You can walk a long time in its peaceful, bourgeois neighborhoods without suspecting that you're in the heart of a city of eight hundred thousand inhabitants.

Suddenly, at the top of an avenue much like the others, we find ourselves on the edge of a cliff with a view of the sea. The road leading down to the plain spread out at our feet is so dizzying that it seems mad to risk it by car. [1954]

Untitled, 1939. Brett Weston.

73

Sunset Streets, 1985. Wayne Thiebaud.

"IT'S CARLO MARX!" SCREAMED DEAN ABOVE THE FURY.

And it was. This little grandmother's boy with the taped-up alto had beady, glittering eyes; small, crooked feet; spindly legs; and he hopped and flopped with his horn and threw his feet around and kept his eyes fixed on the audience (which was just people laughing at a dozen tables, the room thirty by thirty feet and low ceiling), and he never stopped. He was very simple in his ideas. What he liked was the surprise of a new simple variation of a chorus. He'd go from "ta-tup-tader-rara . . . ta-tup-tader-rara," repeating and hopping to it and kissing and smiling into his horn, to "ta-tup-EE-da-de-dera-RUP! ta-tup-EE-da-de-dera-RUP!" and it was all great moments of laughter and understanding for him and everyone else who heard. His tone was clear as a bell, high, pure, and blew straight in our faces from two feet away. Dean stood in front of him, oblivious to everything else in the world, with his head bowed, his hands socking in together, his whole body jumping on his heels and the sweat, always the sweat, pouring and splashing down his tormented collar to lie actually in a pool at his feet. Galatea and Marie were there, and it took us five minutes to realize it. Whoo, Frisco nights, the end of the continent and the end of doubt, all dull doubt and tomfoolery, good-by. [1955]

Two Musicians, 1960. James Weeks.

LITTLE BOXES ON THE HILLSIDE,
Little boxes made of ticky tacky,
Little boxes on the hillside,
Little boxes, all the same.
There's a green one and a pink one
And a blue one and a yellow one
And they're all made out of ticky tacky
And they all look just the same.

And the people in the houses
All went to the university,
Where they were put in boxes,
And they came out all the same,
And there's doctors and there's lawyers
And business executives,
And they're all made out of ticky tacky
And they all look just the same. [1962]

Sunset District and Pacific Ocean, San Francisco, **1951.** Pirkle Jones.
Overleaf: *San Francisco Nova,* **1979.** Robert Bechtle.

JOHN PHILLIPS **SAN FRANCISCO (BE SURE TO WEAR SOME FLOWERS IN YOUR HAIR)**

IF YOU'RE GOING TO SAN FRANCISCO,
Be sure to wear some flowers in your hair.
If you're goin' to San Francisco,
You're gonna meet some gentle people there.

For those who come to San Francisco,
Summertime will be a love-in there.
In the streets of San Francisco,
Gentle people with flowers in their hair.

All across the nation,
Such a strong vibration: People in motion.
There's a whole generation,
with a new explanation, People in motion, People in motion.

If you come to San Francisco,
Summertime will be a love-in there. [1967]

Peace March (detail), 1971. Morrie Camhi.

Peace March, 1971. Morrie Camhi.

KESEY AND THE PRANKSTERS WERE PRIMED FOR THE FESTIVAL. Even Mountain Girl was on hand. She had wrestled the thing out in her mind and was back on the bus. The Pranksters had just held an Acid Test at the Fillmore Auditorium, a big ballroom in the middle of one of San Francisco's big Negro slums, the Fillmore district. It was a wild night. Hundreds of heads and bohos from all over the Bay area turned out, zonked to the eyeballs. Paul Krassner was back in town, and he heard the word that was out on . . . The Scene. Everybody would be "dropping acid" about 5 or 6 P.M. to get ready for the Acid Test to begin that night at nine o'clock at the Fillmore Auditorium. Krassner arrives and—shit!—he sees:

. . . *a ballroom surrealistically seething with a couple of thousand bodies stoned out of their everlovin' bruces in crazy costumes and obscene makeup with a raucous rock 'n' roll band and stroboscopic lights and a thunder machine and balloons and heads and streamers and electronic equipment and the back of a guy's coat proclaiming* Please don't believe in magic *to a girl dancing with 4-inch eyelashes so that even the goddamn Pinkerton Guards were contact high.*

Kesey asks him to take the microphone and contribute to a running commentary on the scene. "All I know," he announces into the din, "is that if I were a cop and I came in here, I wouldn't know where to begin." [1968]

PRESENTED IN SAN FRANCISCO BY BILL GRAHAM

TICKET OUTLETS

San Francisco	Berkeley	Mill Valley
City Lights Book	Discount Records	The Mod Hatter
Psychedelic Shop	Shakespeare & Co.	Sausalito
Baily Lo – Union Square		Rexall Pharmacy
Town Squire – 1318 Polk		

BILL GRAHAM PRESENTS THE SAN FRANCISCO SCENE

JEFFERSON!!
AIRPLANE

GRATEFUL
DEAD

BIG BROTHER
AND THE
HOLDING CO.

LIGHT SHOW BY GLENN MCKAY
HEAD
LIGHTS

AT THE
HOLLYWOOD
BOWL

MAX TELLS ME ABOUT HOW HE AND SHARON GOT TOGETHER. "WHEN I saw her the first time on Haight Street, I flashed. I mean flashed. So I started some conversation with her about her beads, see, but I didn't care about her beads." Sharon lived in a house where a friend of Max's lived, and the next time he saw her was when he took the friend some bananas. "It was during the great banana bubble. You had to kind of force your personality and the banana peels down their throats. Sharon and I were like kids—we just smoked bananas and looked at each other and smoked more bananas and looked at each other."

But Max hesitated. For one thing he thought Sharon was his friend's girl. "For another I didn't know if I wanted to get hung up with an old lady." But the next time he visited the house, Sharon was on acid.

"So everybody yelled 'Here comes the banana man,'" Sharon interrupts, "and I got all excited."

"She was living in this crazy house," Max continues. "There was this one kid, all he did was scream. His whole trip was to practice screams. It was too much." Max still hung back from Sharon. "But then she offered me a tab, and I knew."

Max walked to the kitchen and back with the tab, wondering whether to take it. "And then I decided to flow with it, and that was that. Because once you drop acid with somebody you flash on, you see the whole world melt in her eyes."

"It's stronger than anything in the world," Sharon says.

"Nothing can break it up," Max says. "As long as it lasts." [1966]

San Francisco, 1966–67. William Gedney.

ONLY IN GREECE AND IN THE SINAI HAVE I SEEN LIGHT QUITE AS
three-dimensional, dense, limpid, delicate, dreamlike, and clear: To
say that much of San Francisco faces north over water only partially
explains the effect. I have lived in Haifa, another city that faces north
over water. From its hills one can see extraordinary light, but it is
not like the light of San Francisco. It isn't as rich. The light of Rome
is richer, but it isn't as clear. In Paris, the light does magical things
but only in the sky and among the clouds, seldom descending. San
Francisco light isn't merely bright and glowing like none other; it en-
gages you in its battle with the fog, makes you an ally, sweeps you
along, carries you with it (when you look out over the distance) as if
you were not where you are standing but where you are looking. The
pellucid, enthralling light of San Francisco is like one of those huge
emerald waves in Hawaii through which surprised surfers break only
to find themselves on the covers of magazines.

Light is the soul of San Francisco. It is responsible for the
serenity and inner freedom that are otherwise inexplicable. It ener-
gizes. It enthralls. It redeems bad buildings and jerry-built neighborhoods and makes more beautiful the beautiful buildings and their
surroundings. Most importantly, it, like the laws of proportion, is an
agent that perpetually shapes the city—through human intentions,
but beyond them. Unlike proportion, however, which underlies even the
light itself, the light is something specific, active, and surprising. Once,
I was walking in Fort Mason, under the shade of the trees. I came to a
place on the path where the view gave out on the Golden Gate. The
metal roofs of Fort Mason itself were hardly a shade different from the
color of the bridge; beyond the bridge the cliffs were tinged in red; and
beyond them something was in the air, an almost imperceptible glint
of gold and red light. My line of sight, amplified by the resonance of →

Cityscape I (formerly *Landscape I*), 1963. Richard Diebenkorn.

the otherworldly red and gold, was like the trajectory of a rocket, which is perhaps why I suddenly felt as if I'd been shot out of a cannon. The sensation was that of flight, of tremendous velocity, of moving out of the dark, out of oneself, and into gravityless light. San Francisco is one of the few cities in the world where things like this happen not only to beatitudes and mystics but to newsboys, politicians, and donut-fryers. If it hasn't happened to you, perhaps you should move to Philadelphia.
[1990]

San Francisco from Twin Peaks, ca. 1953, printed ca. 1972. Ansel Adams.

A Tall Building on a Small Lot, Perspective Collage, City Skyline View, 1991. Jim Jennings.

SAN FRANCISCO LAND'S END AND OCEAN'S BEGINNING THE LAND
the sea's edge also The river within us the sea about us The place
where the story ended the place where the story began The first
frontier the last frontier Beginning of end and end of beginning End of
land and land of beginning Embarcadero Freeway to nowhere turned
into part of Vaillancourt's 'Wrecked Freeway Fountain' What is the
water saying to the sea on San Francisco waterfront where I spent
most of my divorce from civilization in and out waterfront hangouts
China Basin Mission Rock Resort Public Fishing Pier Harbor Lunch
Tony's Bayview Red's Java House Shanty Gallery Bottom-of-the-Mark
Eagle Café Longshoreman's Hall the Waterfront dead No Work No Pay
Golden Gate Pilot Boat in fog Podesta Divers SS American Racer rusty
Mystic Mariner Motorship Goy Mount Vernon Victory Red Stack Tugs
standing out past the pier where I telephoned the lawyers saying I
was shipping out on the sailing ship Balclutha and wouldn't be back
until they tore down the Embarcadero Freeway along with the rest of
petroleum civilization and the literary-industrial complex far from where
I'm standing opposite Alcatraz by the thousand fishing boats nested
in green thick water The sea a green god feeding Filipino fishermen on
the quays Hawaiians in baseball caps and peajackets retired Chief
Petty officers casting live bait Puerto Ricans with pile-worms in tincans
Old capital N Negroes with catfish called something else here The
top of Angel Island showing through fog funneled through Golden
Gate Monday morning October sun the Harbor Cruise boat tilting with
tourists into a fogbank Gulls on the roofs of piers asleep in sun The
Last Mohican eating his lunch out of a pail and catching his next lunch
with the last of it The phone booth where I telephoned It's All Over
Count Me Out The fog lifting the sun the sun burning through The →

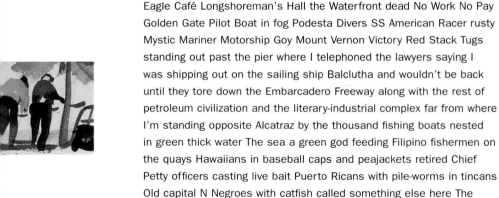

Waterfront, 1937. Dong Kingman.

bright steamers standing out in the end of the first poem I ever wrote in San Francisco twenty years ago just married on a rooftop in North Beach overlooking this place I've come to in this life this waterfront of existence A great view and here comes more life The Western Pacific Freight Ferry ploughing across the horizon between two piers foghorn blowing as I ask a passing elderly ship captain in plaid suit and Tyrolean hat for the time and he takes out his pocket chronometer which says a quarter of two and tells me in thick Norwegian accent 'Quarrter to Tvelve' he just off a plane from Chicago no doubt going to catch his ship for the Far East after visiting his aged mother in Minnesota Foghorns still sounding at the Golden Gate An old freighter light-in-the-water on headings adjusting its compass a pilot flag up and the captain on a wing of the bridge coffeemug in hand greatcoat collar up The wind beginning to come up blowing the fog away from the phone booth the phone dial very clear All of Angel Island now visible through the fogbank A red hull appears standing-in loaded to the gun-nels with oil An Arab on the bridge his turban flying Passing Alcatraz he buys it The Last of the Mohicans reels in his line On the end of it a string of beads once lost in a trade for Manhattan Island The Belt Line Railroad engine stands snorting on a spur next to the Eagle Café with a string of flats & boxcars I park on the tracks imbedded in asphalt and enter the Eagle Café a sign on the wall saying 'Save the Eagle—Last of an Endangered Species' and I get beer just as old brakeman runs in and shouts 'Blue Volkswagen bus!' I rush out and save my bus from the train I see a clock and run for the phone on the pier where the lawyer's supposed to call me back at noon There's a dude in the booth with his address book out and a lot of coins spread out on the ledge He's dialing ten numbers He's putting the coins in very slowly →

San Francisco Project: Inhabiting the Quake, Quake City, 1995. Lebbeus Woods.

101

He starts talking slowly He's really enjoying himself The tide is running
out The Balclutha strains at its moorings The guy in the booth has a lot
to say and lotsa time to say it He's in his own civilized world enclosed
in the booth of civilization and I'm in mine outside waiting for my lawyer
to call back with the final word on my divorce from civilization Will they
let Man be free or won't they Will they or won't they let him be a bar-
barian or a wanderer if he wants to I look at my reflection in the glass
of the phone booth outside It's like a mirror of the world with a wild me
in it and the Bank of America towering over behind me Will Eros or Civilization win And who's this weirdo who is myself and where does he
think he's going to sail away to when there isn't any longer any Away
Another huge oiler stands in All the fucked-up diplomats of the world on
the bridge holding empty champagne glasses as in a Fellini movie The
guy in the booth hangs up and falls out I sit down in the booth and
drink my beer waiting for the phone to ring The Balclutha's whistle
blows The tide is at the ebb The phone rings [1976]

San Francisco Wharfs, 1937. Sonya Noskowiak.
Overleaf: *Ship's Bow, SF Skyline, Interstate 80,* 1982. Richard Lohmann.

103

ALL THINGS CONSIDERED, HALLOWEEN WEEKEND HAD GONE QUITE WELL.
So far.

Michael's parents had rented a Dodge Aspen upon their arrival
in the city, so it was easy enough to fill up their time with Muir Woods
and Sausalito, The Crooked Street and Fisherman's Wharf.

But now it was Sunday. The Witches' Sabbath was upon them.

If he was careful, very careful, he could ease them through it,
protect their fragile, *Reader's Digest* sensibilities from the horror of
The Love That Dares Not Speak Its Name.

Maybe.

In *this* town, he thought, The Love That Dares Not Speak Its
Name almost never shuts up. . . .

* * *

The Aspen was parked up on Leavenworth, near Green. Michael's
mother was out of breath by the time they reached Union. "I've never
seen a street like that in my life, Mikey!"

He squeezed her arm, taking sudden pleasure in her innocence.
"It's an amazing city, Mama."

Almost on cue, the nuns appeared.

"Herb, look!"

"Goddammit, Alice! Don't point!"

"Herb . . . they're on roller skates!"

"Goddamn if they aren't! Mike, what the hell . . . ?"

Before their son could answer, the six white-coifed figures had
rounded the corner as a unit, rocketing in the direction of the revelry
on Polk Street.

One of them bellowed at Michael.

"Hey, Tolliver!"

Michael waved half-heartedly.

The nun gave a high sign, blew a kiss, then shouted: "*Loved* your
jockey shorts!" [1978]

Mars Alley, San Francisco, 1984. John Harding.

SAN FRANCISCO, AUGUST 31, 1866.

Looking over the latest copy of the *Republican* received by mail, I begin to recognize a certain fitness in your having a representative from this coast among your correspondents. I can at least offer a relief to the monotony of their meteorological observations. While they, along the Atlantic seaboard, sing an unvarying "song of heat," and bear equal testimony to scorching skies, shades that are grateful, and brooks whose murmur the sultry atmosphere makes delicious, perhaps it is well that you have on this Pacific slope an exception to that isothermal crew—one sternly truthful and sadly sincere man, who can, out of his own experience, paint the opposite of that evenly charming picture; who could if he liked literally throw a wet blanket over their bucolic efforts. . . . Where else can one so perfectly fulfill the real conditions of existence—eating, drinking, sleeping and working— as here?

Ought I not to be thankful that I can sleep under blankets instead of being driven to the necessity of celestial contemplation from an open window, through the extreme heat of a summer's night? Should I not be satisfied that I can work the summer through without needing vacation, instead of idling away a month or two in dreaming by babbling brooks or under whispering trees? Or, food being the question, I am pointed to the market, where Pomona has, in the reckless fashion in which everything is done here, poured out her stores in golden and purple grapes, nectarines, apricots and peaches, apples, pears and quinces, which heap the stalls in this damp, grey, autumnal weather. And here are watermelons! Watermelons, and the fog enveloping you like a wet sheet. Watermelons on your table, and a fire in your dining-room. Nature revolts and the blood curdles at the thought. →

Fog over Twin Peaks, San Francisco, 1955. Pirkle Jones.

Let me be generous. We have had two days of clear weather, and the winds comparatively unobjectionable. But let me also be just. An old resident answered my congratulations with a dubious shake of the head, "Earthquake weather!" Nothing I can say here can equal this unconscious satire on the San Francisco climate. To be forced to look upon a fine day as abnormal and ominous, and to apprehend compensation in a general convulsion of the earth's surface, reveals a condition of things that even in my bitterest moments I have never yet ventured to express. [1866]

Alcoa Building, Montgomery Street, San Francisco, 1968. Kenneth Graves.
Overleaf: *Sand Dunes and Fog, San Francisco*, early 1880s. William Keith.

THEY PARK THE CAR BY THE MARINA.
The surface of the cobalt bay
Is flecked with white. The moister, keener
October air has rinsed away
The whispering mists with crisp intensity
And over the opaque immensity
A deliquescent wash of blue
Reveals the bridge, long lost to view
In summer's quilt of fog: the towers
High-built, red-gold, with their long span
—The most majestic spun by man—
Whose threads of steel through mists and showers,
Wind, spray, and the momentous roar
Of ocean storms, link shore to shore. [1986]

Reflected San Francisco Beauty Spots, 1979. Iain Baxter.

BUT IT WAS THAT BEAUTIFUL CUT OF CLOUDS I COULD ALWAYS SEE above the little S.P. alley, puffs floating by from Oakland or the Gate of Marin to the north or San Jose south, the clarity of Cal to break your heart. It was the fantastic drowse and drum hum of lum mum afternoon nathin' to do, ole Frisco with end of land sadness—the people—the alley full of trucks and cars of businesses nearabouts and nobody knew or far from cared who I was all my life three thousand five hundred miles from birth-O opened up and at last belonged to me in Great America. [1957]

City Tracks, 1988. Willard Dixon.

IF YOU HAPPEN TO BE ENDOWED WITH TOPOGRAPHICAL CURIOSITY
the hills of San Francisco fill you with an irresistible desire to walk to
the top of each one of them. Whoever laid the town out took the con-
ventional checkerboard pattern of streets and without the slightest
regard for the laws of gravity planked it down blind on an irregular
peninsula that was a confusion of steep slopes and sandhills. The
result is exhilarating. Wherever you step out on the street there's a
hilltop in one direction or the other. From the top of each hill you get
a view and the sight of more hills to the right and left and ahead that
offer the prospect of still broader views. The process goes on indefi-
nitely. You can't help making your way painfully to the top of each hill
just to see what you can see. [1944]

SOME YEARS AGO, EXPLORING THE ROCKY SHORELINE NEAR THE Cliff House during an extraordinarily low tide, I clambered over a boulder just in time to escape an incoming breaker and found myself in a hidden cove facing what appeared to be the ruins of an ancient palace. It was Sutro Baths, for half a century one of San Francisco's prime recreation spots. Winds, waves, and vandals had broken nearly every one of the hundreds of panes of glass that faced the ocean. I walked across a beach left bare by the minus tide, scrambled up the sea wall, and peered inside.

The floor of the hangar-sized room was terraced back up the hillside, and on the lower levels were five empty swimming pools of various sizes and shapes. The long pool nearest the window was partly filled with sand where storm breakers had swept inside the building. In a sudden flashback, there came to me a recollection of the last time I had swum here many years earlier. The vast pavilion was filled with the shouts of hundreds of bathers and the music of Strauss waltzes. On the upper terraces, behind seats where thousands of spectators had once watched Duke Kahanamoku slice through the water for one hundred yards to set a new world's record, were acres of tropical vegetation, palms, big-leaved vines, exotic flowers, classic plaster statues and huge stuffed animals—all in delightful Victorian array.

The pools themselves were a wonder. You could plummet into the water from diving platforms up in the rafters; rocket into the pools down giddy slides that seemed to come down from the roof; whirl into the water from a carousel; swing out over the pools on trapeze-like rings attached to the ceiling. In memory, at least, these were pools to surpass the fabled spas of Europe and the Lucullan baths of the Roman emperors. [1972]

Sutro Baths: A New Public Room: Hillside View, 1991. William Leddy.

NO MORE JAZZ
At Alcatraz
No more piano
for Lucky Luciano
No more trombone
for Al Capone
No more jazz
at Alcatraz
No more cello
for Frank Costello
No more screeching of the
Seagulls
As they line up for
Chow
No more jazz
At Alcatraz [n.d.]

Alcatraz, 1988. Jo Babcock.

MARIA PAZ LAUGHS. "BUT IT WAS A *BRIDGE*, DARLING. PEOPLE drove back and forth in cars, from one end to the other." She laughs again. "There were too many cars, finally, so they dug the tunnels under the Bay. Tunnels for the cars, tunnels for the maglevs. The bridge was old, in need of repair. They closed it, but then the devaluations began, the depression. There was no money for the repairs they'd planned. The bridge stood empty. And then one night, as if someone had given a signal, the homeless came. But the legend is that there *was* no signal. People simply *came*. They climbed the chainlink and the barricades at either end; they climbed in such num-bers that the chainlink twisted and fell. They tumbled the concrete barricades into the Bay. They climbed the towers. Dozens died, falling to their deaths. But when dawn came, they were here, on the bridge, clinging, claiming it, and the cities, dear," she blew twin streams of smoke from her nostrils, "knew that the world was watching. They were no longer invisible, you see, the homeless people; they'd come together on this span of steel, had claimed it as their own. The cities had to be cautious then. Already the Japanese were preparing an airlift of food and medical supplies. A national embarrassment. No time for the water cannon, no. They were allowed to stay. Temporarily. The first structures were of cardboard." Maria Paz smiles.

"Skinner? You think he came then?"

"Perhaps. If he's as old as you seem to think he is. How long have you been on the bridge, dear?"

"Three months, maybe."

"I was born here," says Maria Paz. [1990]

Untitled, **1989. Hodgetts and Fung.**

Left: *Tightening Catwalk Bolts, Five Passing Ferries*, 1935. Peter Stackpole.
Right: *Cable Saddle, Bay Bridge*, 1935. Peter Stackpole.

The Lone Riveter, 1935. Peter Stackpole.

Left: *Catwalks, Towers, and Ferryboat People,* 1935. Peter Stackpole.
Right: *Waiting for Rivets and Steel,* 1935. Peter Stackpole.

WHEN I WAS A CHILD GROWING UP IN SALINAS WE CALLED SAN Francisco "the City." Of course it was the only city we knew, but I still think of it as the City, and so does everyone else who has ever associated with it. A strange and exclusive word is "city." Besides San Francisco, only small sections of London and Rome stay in the mind as the City. New Yorkers say they are going to town. Paris has no title but Paris. Mexico City is the Capital.

Once I knew the City very well, spent my attic days there, while others were being a lost generation in Paris. I fledged in San Francisco, climbed its hills, slept in its parks, worked on its docks, marched and shouted in its revolts. In a way I felt I owned the City as much as it owned me.

San Francisco put on a show for me. I saw her across the bay, from the great road that bypasses Sausalito and enters the Golden Gate Bridge. The afternoon sun painted her white and gold—rising on her hills like a noble city in a happy dream. A city on hills has it over flat-land places. New York makes its own hills with craning buildings, but this gold and white acropolis rising wave on wave against the blue of the Pacific sky was a stunning thing, a painted thing like a picture of a medieval Italian city which can never have existed. I stopped in a parking place to look at her and the necklace bridge over the entrance from the sea that led to her. Over the green higher hills to the south, the evening fog rolled like herds of sheep coming to cote in the golden city. I've never seen her more lovely. When I was a child and we were going to the City, I couldn't sleep for several nights before, out of bursting excitement. She leaves a mark. [1961]

View of the Bay Bridge, 2000. Larry Cohen.

THO I DIE ON A DISTANT STRAND,
And they give me a grave in that land,
    Yet carry me back to my own city!
    Carry me back to her grace and pity!
For I think I could not rest
Afar from her mighty breast.
She is fairer than others are
    Whom they sing the beauty of.
Her heart is a song and a star—
    My cool, grey city of love.

Tho they tear the rose from her brow,
To her is ever my vow;
    Ever to her I give my duty—
    First in rapture and first in beauty,
Wayward, passionate, brave,
Glad of the life God gave.
The sea-winds are her kiss,
    And the sea-gull is her dove;
Cleanly and strong she is—
    My cool, grey city of love. →

Ferry Building, San Francisco, ca. 1910. Xavier Martinez.

The winds of the Future wait
At the iron walls of her Gate,
    And the western ocean breaks in thunder,
    And the western stars go slowly under,
And her gaze is ever West
In the dream of her young unrest.
Her sea is a voice that calls,
    And her star a voice above,
And her wind a voice on her walls—
    My cool, grey city of love.

Tho they stay her feet at the dance,
In her is the far romance.
    Under the rain of winter falling,
    Vine and rose will await recalling.
Tho the dark be cold and blind,
Yet her sea-fog's touch is kind,
And her mightier caress
    Is joy and the pain thereof;
And great is thy tenderness,
    O cool, grey city of love! [1920]

Breaking Wave, Golden Gate, San Francisco, 1952, printed 1968. Pirkle Jones.

FRONT COVER
Gabriel Moulin
San Francisco
1935
gelatin silver print
9 ^{1}/8 x 7 ^{1}/4 in. (23.2 x 18.4 cm)
The Prentice and Paul Sack Photographic
Trust of the San Francisco Museum of
Modern Art, ST1998.0346

BACK COVER
Wayne Thiebaud
Bright City
1993
acrylic on canvas
36 x 24 in. (91.4 x 61 cm)
San Francisco Museum of Modern Art,
fractional and promised gift of Vicki and
Kent Logan, 97.879

FRONT ENDSHEET
Brett Weston
Untitled (detail)
1939
gelatin silver print
7 ^{5}/8 x 9 ^{5}/8 in. (19.4 x 24.5 cm)
San Francisco Museum of Modern Art,
gift of Mrs. Drew Chidester, 59.2102

BACK ENDSHEET
Jim Jennings
*A Tall Building on a Small Lot, Perspec-
tive Collage, City Skyline View*
(detail)
1991
hand-colored photocopy on paper
13 x 35 ^{1}/2 in. (33 x 90.2 cm)
San Francisco Museum of Modern Art,
gift of the Office of Jim Jennings,
95.206

FRONTISPIECE
Unknown
Aerial View of San Francisco
1970
gelatin silver print
26 ^{3}/4 x 26 ^{13}/16 in. (68 x 68.1 cm)
San Francisco Museum of Modern Art,
gift of Gordon L. Bennett, 96.195

Ansel Adams
*The Golden Gate Before the Bridge,
San Francisco, California*
ca. 1932, printed ca. 1972
gelatin silver print
15 ^{5}/16 x 19 ^{1}/8 in. (38.9 x 48.6 cm)
San Francisco Museum of Modern Art,
gift of Alfred Fromm, Otto Meyer, and
Louis Petri, San Francisco, 74.52.17

Charles Sheeler
Golden Gate
1955
oil on canvas
25 x 34 in. (63.5 x 86.4 cm)
The Metropolitan Museum of Art,
New York, George A. Hearn Fund, 1955
(55.99)

Arthur Ollman
Untitled
1979
Ektacolor print
8 ^{11}/16 x 13 in. (22.1 x 33 cm)
San Francisco Museum of Modern Art,
gift of Dr. and Mrs. William R. Fielder,
84.206

Arthur Mathews
*Discovery of the Bay of San Francisco by
Portolá*
1896
oil on canvas
70 ^{1}/4 x 58 ^{1}/2 in. (178.4 x 148.6 cm)
Courtesy Garzoli Gallery, San Rafael,
California

Ansel Adams
*Marin Hills, over the Golden Gate from
Lincoln Park, San Francisco*
ca. 1950, printed ca. 1972
gelatin silver print
14 ^{7}/8 x 19 ^{1}/8 in. (37.8 x 48.6 cm)
San Francisco Museum of Modern Art,
gift of Alfred Fromm, Otto Meyer, and
Louis Petri, San Francisco, 74.52.23

Victor Prevost (attrib.)
Yerba Buena, 1847
1847
oil on canvas
25 x 30 in. (63.5 x 76.2 cm)
California Historical Society, gift of the
Ohio Historical Society

Raymond Dabb Yelland
San Francisco from Goat Island
1881
oil on canvas
12 x 28 ^{1}/4 in. (30.5 x 71.8 cm)
Oakland Museum of California, gift of
Mr. and Mrs Herbert M. Stoll, Jr.

Joan Brown
The Dancers in a City #2
1972
enamel and fabric on canvas
84 x 71 ^{3}/4 in. (213.4 x 182.3 cm)
San Francisco Museum of Modern Art,
gift of Alfred E. Heller, 80.407

George Henry Burgess
San Francisco in July, 1849
1891
oil on canvas
62 x 132 ^{3}/4 in. (157.5 x 337 cm)
Oakland Museum of California, gift of
the Women's Board

Willard E. Worden
Admission Day
1909
gelatin silver print
7 ^{9}/16 x 9 ^{9}/16 in. (19.2 x 24.3 cm)
San Francisco Museum of Modern Art,
Accessions Committee Fund, 98.290

Unknown
Studio Portrait in front of Cliff House
1880s or 1890s
quarter-plate tintype
3 ^{1}/2 x 2 ^{1}/2 in. (8.9 x 6.4 cm)
The Prentice and Paul Sack Photographic
Trust of the San Francisco Museum of
Modern Art, ST1998.0543.5

Adolf Dittmer
Untitled
1905, printed 1967
gelatin silver print
5 ^{13}/16 x 7 ^{3}/4 in. (14.8 x 19.7 cm)
San Francisco Museum of Modern Art,
gift of Herb Quick, 69.7

Carleton E. Watkins
Golden Gate, San Francisco, number
669 from the *Pacific Coast* series
1867
stereograph
3 x 6 in. (7.6 x 15.2 cm)
The Prentice and Paul Sack Photographic
Trust of the San Francisco Museum of
Modern Art, ST1998.0566

Willard E. Worden
Ships on the Bay, Golden Gate
1904
gelatin silver print
3 ^{15}/16 x 9 ^{13}/16 in. (10 x 24.9 cm)
San Francisco Museum of Modern Art,
gift of Robert Harshorn Shimshak,
84.1539

William Hahn
*Market Scene, Sansome Street,
San Francisco*
1872
oil on canvas
60 x 96 in. (152.4 x 243.8 cm)
E. B. Crocker Collection, Crocker Art
Museum, Sacramento, California

Arnold Genthe
Untitled, from *The San Francisco
Earthquake and Fire*
1906
glass lantern slide
4 x 5 in. (10.2 x 12.7 cm)
San Francisco Museum of Modern Art,
in memory of Harry H. Lunn, gift of the
Robert Mann Gallery, 2000.188.46

Arnold Genthe
Untitled, from *The San Francisco
Earthquake and Fire*
1906
glass lantern slide
4 x 5 in. (10.2 x 12.7 cm)
San Francisco Museum of Modern Art,
in memory of Harry H. Lunn, gift of the
Robert Mann Gallery, 2000.188.34

Arnold Genthe
*Looking up Market Street towards
Twin Peaks*
1906
gelatin silver print
8 x 10 in. (20.3 x 25.4 cm)
The Prentice and Paul Sack Photographic
Trust of the San Francisco Museum of
Modern Art, ST1998.0188

Arnold Genthe
Untitled, from *The San Francisco
Earthquake and Fire*
1906
glass lantern slide
4 x 5 in. (10.2 x 12.7 cm)
San Francisco Museum of Modern Art,
in memory of Harry H. Lunn, gift of the
Robert Mann Gallery, 2000.188.40

Arnold Genthe
Untitled
1906
gelatin silver print
7 ^{1}/2 x 9 ^{1}/2 in. (19.1 x 24.1 cm)
San Francisco Museum of Modern Art,
gift of Robert Koch, 88.597

P. Douglas Andersen
A Corner in Chinatown S.F.
ca. 1923
gelatin silver print
11 ^{7}/16 x 9 ^{5}/16 in. (29.1 x 23.7 cm)
San Francisco Museum of Modern Art,
purchase, 78.13

Colin Campbell Cooper
The Palace of Fine Arts
1916
oil on canvas
40 ^{1}/4 x 50 in. (102.2 x 127 cm)
Crocker Art Museum, Sacramento,
California, gift of Miss Helen Seeley in
memory of Mr. and Mrs. C. C. Cooper.
Conserved with funds provided by Mr.
Gerald D. Gordon through the Gifts to
Share program

Unknown
Untitled, from an album of Panama
Pacific International Exposition
photographs
1915
gelatin silver print
8 x 6 ^{1}/16 in. (20.3 x 15.4 cm)
The Prentice and Paul Sack Photographic
Trust of the San Francisco Museum of
Modern Art, ST1998.0504.BBB

Unknown
Untitled, from an album of Panama
Pacific International Exposition
photographs
1915
gelatin silver print
6 ^{1}/8 x 7 ^{15}/16 in. (15.6 x 20.2 cm)
The Prentice and Paul Sack Photographic
Trust of the San Francisco Museum of
Modern Art, ST1998.0504.HHH

Alfred Bendiner
From Nob Hill
n.d.
watercolor
26 ^{1}/8 in. x 40 in. (66.7 x 101.6 cm)
San Francisco Museum of Modern Art,
gift of the Alfred Bendiner Foundation,
87.36

Max Yavno
Cable Car
n.d.
gelatin silver print
15 ^{7}/8 x 19 ^{7}/8 in. (40.3 x 50.5 cm)
San Francisco Museum of Modern Art,
gift of the Estate of Max Yavno, 89.49

Max Yavno
Untitled
1947
gelatin silver print
5 x 6 ^{3}/4 in. (12.7 x 17.2 cm)
San Francisco Museum of Modern Art,
gift of A. Justin Sterling, 85.570

Dong Kingman
Untitled
n.d.
watercolor on paper
18 x 22 ^{3}/4 in. (45.7 x 57.8 cm)
San Francisco Museum of Modern Art,
gift of Rocky Aoki from the Benihana
Collection, 84.197

Dorothea Lange
*Five Workers against Concrete Wall,
Industrial District, San Francisco*
1933
gelatin silver print
9 ^{1}/2 x 9 ^{5}/8 in. (24.1 x 24.5 cm)
San Francisco Museum of Modern Art,
Accessions Committee Fund, 93.212

John Gutmann
Nob Hill, San Francisco
1938, printed ca. 1974
gelatin silver print
8 x 10 in. (20.3 x 25.4 cm)
San Francisco Museum of Modern Art,
bequest of John Gutmann, 2000.344

Elmer Bischoff
Yellow Lampshade
1969
oil on canvas
70 x 80 in. (177.8 x 203.2 cm)
Fine Arts Museum of San Francisco, gift
of Nan Tucker McEvoy, in memory of her
mother, Phyllis de Young Tucker, 1992.10

Dorothea Lange
San Francisco Strike
1933
gelatin silver print
9 ^{1}/8 x 7 ^{1}/4 in. (23.2 x 18.4 cm)
San Francisco Museum of Modern Art.
The Henry Swift Collection. Gift of
Florence Alston Swift, 63.19.127

Fletcher Martin
Trouble in Frisco
n.d.
lithograph
15 ^{7}/8 x 13 ^{15}/16 in. (40.3 x 35.4 cm)
San Francisco Museum of Modern Art.
Albert M. Bender Collection. Gift of
Albert M. Bender, 37.864

Robert Frank
San Francisco
1955–66
gelatin silver print
18 ⁵/₈ in. x 12 ¹/₈ in. (47.3 x 30.8 cm)
Courtesy of the artist and Pace/MacGill
Gallery

Brett Weston
Untitled
1939
gelatin silver print
7 ⁵/₈ x 9 ⁵/₈ in. (19.4 x 24.5 cm)
San Francisco Museum of Modern Art,
gift of Mrs. Drew Chidester, 59.2102

Wayne Thiebaud
Sunset Streets
1985
oil on canvas
48 x 35 ³/₄ in. (121.9 x 90.8 cm)
San Francisco Museum of Modern Art,
purchased with the aid of funds from
public subscription, William L. Gerstle
Fund, Fund of the '80s, Clinton Walker
Fund, and Thomas W. Weisel, 86.6

James Weeks
Two Musicians
1960
oil on canvas
84 x 66 in. (213.4 x 167.6 cm)
San Francisco Museum of Modern Art,
Thomas W. Weisel Fund purchase,
84.127

Pirkle Jones
*Sunset District and Pacific Ocean, San
Francisco, from Portfolio Two, Twelve
Photographs by Pirkle Jones*
1951
gelatin silver print
9 ³/₈ x 13 ¹/₄ in. (23.8 x 33.7 cm)
San Francisco Museum of Modern Art,
acquired through purchase and
exchange, 70.40.5

Robert Bechtle
San Francisco Nova
1979
oil on canvas
46 x 69 in. (116.8 x 175.3 cm)
Collection of the City and County of San
Francisco; courtesy of the San Francisco
Arts Commission, 1979.59

Morrie Camhi
Peace March
1971
gelatin silver print
6 ¹/₄ x 13 ⁵/₈ in. (15.9 x 34.6 cm)
San Francisco Museum of Modern Art,
bequest of Helen Johnston, 90.125

Karen Calden Fulk
Psychedelic Leather Pants
1971
cowhide, dye, stitching
37 x 20 x ¹/₂ in. (93.9 x 50.8 x 1.3 cm)
San Francisco Museum of Modern Art,
gift of Karen Calden Fulk, aka: Karen C.
Jones, 98.343

Wes Wilson
*The Association, Quicksilver Messenger
Service—Fillmore Auditorium, July
22–23, 1966*
1966
offset lithograph
20 ⁵/₈ x 13 ⁷/₈ in. (52.4 x 35.2 cm)
San Francisco Museum of Modern Art,
gift of Jim Chanin, 95.630

Jim Blashfield
*Jefferson Airplane, Grateful Dead—
Hollywood Bowl, September 15, 1967*
1967
offset lithograph
20 x 13 ⁷/₈ in. (50.8 x 35.2 cm)
San Francisco Museum of Modern Art,
gift of Jim Chanin, 95.693

William Gedney
San Francisco
1966–67
gelatin silver print
12 x 8 ¹/₂ in. (30.5 x 21.6 cm)
San Francisco Museum of Modern Art,
gift of Duke University Rare Book, Manu-
script, and Special Collections Library
and Gallery 292, NYC, 99.616

Richard Diebenkorn
Cityscape I (formerly *Landscape I*)
1963
oil on canvas
60 ¹/₄ x 50 ¹/₂ in. (153 x 128.3 cm)
San Francisco Museum of Modern Art,
purchased with funds from Trustees and
Friends in memory of Hector Escobosa,
Brayton Wilbur, and J. D. Zellerbach,
64.46

Ansel Adams
San Francisco from Twin Peaks
ca. 1953, printed ca. 1972
gelatin silver print
15 ⁵/₈ x 19 ¹/₂ in. (39.7 x 49.5 cm)
San Francisco Museum of Modern Art,
gift of Alfred Fromm, Otto Meyer, and
Louis Petri, San Francisco, 74.52.15

Jim Jennings
*A Tall Building on a Small Lot, Perspec-
tive Collage, City Skyline View*
1991
hand-colored photocopy on paper
13 x 35 ¹/₂ in. (33 x 90.2 cm)
San Francisco Museum of Modern Art,
gift of the Office of Jim Jennings,
95.206

Dong Kingman
Waterfront
1937
watercolor on paper
19 ³/₄ x 27 in. (50.2 x 68.6 cm)
San Francisco Museum of Modern Art.
William L. Gerstle Collection. William L.
Gerstle Fund Purchase, 41.3107

Lebbeus Woods
*San Francisco Project: Inhabiting the
Quake, Quake City*
1995
pencil and pastel on paper mounted on
board
14 ¹/₂ x 23 x ³/₄ in.
(36.8 x 58.4 x 1.9 cm)
San Francisco Museum of Modern Art,
Accessions Committee Fund, 96.88

Sonya Noskowiak
San Francisco Wharfs
1937
gelatin silver print
7 ¹/₂ x 9 ¹/₂ in. (19.1 x 24.1 cm)
San Francisco Museum of Modern Art,
WPA/FAP Allocation, 65.2.642

Richard Lohmann
Ship's Bow, SF Skyline, Interstate 80,
from the portfolio *Meniscus*
1982
gelatin silver print
4 ³/₄ x 6 ³/₄ in. (12.1 x 17.2 cm)
San Francisco Museum of Modern Art,
donated in memory of Mr. Henry Holmes
Smith, 86.106.8

John Harding
Mars Alley, San Francisco
1984
Ektacolor print
16 x 20 in. (40.7 x 50.8 cm)
San Francisco Museum of Modern Art,
purchase, 88.42

Pirkle Jones
Fog over Twin Peaks, San Francisco
1955
gelatin silver print
9 ⁷/₁₆ x 13 ⁷/₁₆ in. (24 x 34.1 cm)
San Francisco Museum of Modern Art,
gift of Van Deren Coke, 79.179

Kenneth Graves
Alcoa Building, Montgomery Street,
San Francisco
1968
gelatin silver print
7 $^1/_8$ x 10 $^9/_{16}$ in. (18.1 x 26.8 cm)
San Francisco Museum of Modern Art,
gift of the artist, 71.53.3

William Keith
Sand Dunes and Fog, San Francisco
early 1880s
oil on canvas mounted on board
14 x 24 in. (35.6 x 61 cm)
Hearst Art Gallery, Saint Mary's College
of California, gift of Mary B. Alexander
in memory of her husband, Wallace
Alexander

Iain Baxter
Reflected San Francisco Beauty Spots
1979
photo etching and aquatint
34 x 29 $^5/_8$ in. (86.4 x 75.2 cm)
San Francisco Museum of Modern Art,
purchased with the aid of funds from
the Ruth and Moses Lasky Fund and the
Byron Meyer Fund, 79.295.2

Willard Dixon
City Tracks
1988
oil on canvas
43 x 72 in. (109.2 x 182.9 cm)
San Francisco Museum of Modern Art,
gift of Dr. William C. Sawyer, 89.197

Rigo 98
Study for *Looking at 1998 San Francisco*
from the Top of 1925
1998
marker on xerox paper
46 x 66 in. (116.8 x 167.6 cm)
San Francisco Museum of Modern Art,
Ruth Nash Fund purchase, 99.225

William Leddy—Tanner Leddy Maytum
Stacy Architects
Sutro Baths: A New Public Room:
Hillside View
1991
ink on mylar over composite photostats
24 x 19 in. (60.9 x 48.3 cm)
San Francisco Museum of Modern Art,
gift of Tanner Leddy Maytum Stacy
Architects, 95.221

Jo Babcock
Alcatraz
1988
Type C print
49 $^1/_4$ x 40 $^3/_4$ in. (125.1 x 103.5 cm)
San Francisco Museum of Modern Art,
purchased through a gift of Anne Marie
MacDonald, 89.137

Hodgetts and Fung
Untitled
1989
ink and electrostatic print on paper
5 $^9/_{16}$ x 7 $^3/_4$ in. (14.1 x 19.7 cm)
San Francisco Museum of Modern Art,
commissioned for the exhibition *Visionary*
San Francisco, 97.2

Peter Stackpole
Tightening Catwalk Bolts, Five Passing Fer-
ries, from the portfolio *When They Built*
the Bridge: Photographs of the San Fran-
cisco-Oakland Bay Bridge, 1934–1936
1935
gelatin silver print
6 $^3/_8$ x 9 $^1/_2$ in. (16.2 x 24.1 cm)
San Francisco Museum of Modern Art,
gift of Ursula Gropper, 86.136.12

Peter Stackpole
Cable Saddle, Bay Bridge
1935
gelatin silver print
6 $^{15}/_{16}$ x 9 $^1/_8$ in. (17.6 x 23.2 cm)
San Francisco Museum of Modern Art.
The Henry Swift Collection. Gift of
Florence Alston Swift, 63.19.157

Peter Stackpole
The Lone Riveter, from the portfolio
When They Built the Bridge: Photographs
of the San Francisco-Oakland Bay Bridge,
1934–1936
1935
gelatin silver print
9 $^{13}/_{16}$ x 6 $^7/_8$ in. (25 x 17.5 cm)
San Francisco Museum of Modern Art,
gift of Ursula Gropper, 86.136.17

Peter Stackpole
Catwalks, Towers, and Ferryboat People,
from the portfolio *When They Built the*
Bridge: Photographs of the San Francisco-
Oakland Bay Bridge, 1934–1936
1935
gelatin silver print
6 $^1/_2$ x 9 $^3/_4$ in. (16.5 x 24.8 cm)
San Francisco Museum of Modern Art,
gift of Ursula Gropper, 86.136.14

Peter Stackpole
Waiting for Rivets and Steel, from the
portfolio *When They Built the Bridge:*
Photographs of the San Francisco-
Oakland Bay Bridge, 1934–1936
1935
gelatin silver print
6 $^{15}/_{16}$ x 9 $^3/_8$ in. (17.6 x 23.8 cm)
San Francisco Museum of Modern Art,
gift of Ursula Gropper, 86.136.13

Larry Cohen
View of the Bay Bridge
2000
oil on canvas
42 x 42 in. (106.7 x 106.7 cm)
Collection of the artist, courtesy
of Hackett-Freedman Gallery

Xavier Martinez
Ferry Building, San Francisco
ca. 1910
oil on canvas
20 x 24 $^1/_2$ in. (50.8 x 62.2 cm)
Oakland Museum of California, gift
of Miss Laetitia Meyer

Pirkle Jones
Breaking Wave, Golden Gate,
San Francisco
1952, printed 1968
gelatin silver print
9 $^1/_4$ x 13 $^1/_4$ in. (23.5 x 33.7 cm)
San Francisco Museum of Modern Art,
purchase (Accessions Committee Fund
and exchange of reproductions), 70.40.1

Sandow Birk
Scene from the Desolation: San
Francisco Museum of Modern Art
1995
acrylic on canvas
12 $^1/_8$ x 15 $^1/_8$ in. (30.8 x 38.4 cm)
San Francisco Museum of Modern Art,
Ruth Nash Fund purchase, 97.491

TEXTS

Isabel Allende, excerpt from *Daughter of Fortune: A Novel*, translated by Margaret Sayers Peden. Copyright © 1999 by Isabel Allende. English translation copyright © 1999 by HarperCollins Publishers, Inc. Reprinted with the permission of HarperCollins Publishers, Inc. • Maya Angelou, excerpt from *I Know Why the Caged Bird Sings*. Copyright © 1969 by Maya Angelou. Reprinted with the permission of Random House, Inc. • Mary Austin, excerpt from "The Land of the Little Duck" from *California: The Land of the Sun* (New York: The Macmillan Company, 1914). • Simone de Beauvoir, excerpt from *America Day by Day*, translated by Carol Cosman. Copyright 1954 by Éditions Gallimard, Paris. Translation copyright © 1998 by The Regents of the University of California. Reprinted with the permission of University of California Press. • Miguel Costansó, "Thursday, 2 November" from *The Discovery of San Francisco Bay: The Portolá Expedition of 1769–1779: The Diary of Miguel Costansó in Spanish and English*, edited by Peter Browning. Copyright © 1992 by Peter Browning. Reprinted with the permission of Great West Books, P.O. Box 1028, Lafayette, CA 94549. • Richard Henry Dana, excerpt from "Twenty-four Years After," from *Two Years Before the Mast; Twenty-four Years After* (London: J. M. Dent & Sons Ltd, 1969). • Joan Didion, excerpt from *Slouching towards Bethlehem*. Copyright © 1966, 1968 and renewed 1996 by Joan Didion. Reprinted with the permission of Farrar,

Straus & Giroux, LLC. • John Dos Passos, excerpt from "San Francisco Looks West: The City in Wartime" from *Harper's Magazine* (March 1944): 329. Reprinted by permission of Lucy Dos Passos Coggin. • Lawrence Ferlinghetti, "Great American Waterfront Poem" from *Who Are We Now?* Copyright © 1976 by Lawrence Ferlinghetti. Reprinted with the permission of New Directions Publishing Corporation. • William Gibson, excerpt from "Skinner's Room" from *Visionary San Francisco* (San Francisco: San Francisco Museum of Modern Art, 1990). Copyright © 1990 by William Gibson. Reprinted with the permission of the Martha Millard Literary Agency. • Harold Gilliam, excerpt from "The Lost Roman Baths of Adolph Sutro" from *The San Francisco Experience: The Romantic Lore Behind the Fabulous Facade of the Bay Area* (New York: Doubleday, 1972). Copyright © 1972 by Harold Gilliam. Reprinted with the permission of the author. • Dashiell Hammett, excerpt from *The Maltese Falcon*. Copyright 1929, 1930 by Alfred A. Knopf, Inc., renewed © 1957, 1958 by Dashiell Hammett. Reprinted with the permission of Alfred A. Knopf, a division of Random House, Inc. • Bret Harte, excerpt from "*Springfield Republican*, October 6, 1866: Letter from San Francisco" from *San Francisco in 1866: Being Letters to the Springfield Republican*, edited by George R. Stewart and Edwin S. Fussell (San Francisco: The Book Club of California, 1951). • Mark Helprin, excerpt from "The True Builders of Cities" from *Visionary San Francisco* (San Francisco: San Francisco Museum

of Modern Art, 1990). Copyright © 1990 by Mark Helprin. Reprinted with the permission of the author. • Gus Kahn, "San Francisco." Copyright 1936 by Robbins Music Corporation. All rights reserved. • Bob Kaufman, "No More Jazz at Alcatraz" from *Cranial Guitar: Selected Poems*. Copyright © 1996 by Eileen Kaufman. Reprinted with the permission of Coffee House Press. • Jack Kerouac, excerpt from *On the Road*. Copyright © 1955, 1957 by Jack Kerouac, renewed 1985 by Stella Kerouac and Jan Kerouac. Reprinted with the permission of Viking Penguin, a division of Penguin Putnam, Inc. • Jack Kerouac, "October in the Railroad Earth" from *Evergreen Review Reader 1957–1967*, edited by Barney Rosset (New York: Grove, 1968). Copyright © 1957 by Jack Kerouac. Reprinted with the permission of Sterling Lord Literistic, Inc. • Maxine Hong Kingston, excerpt from "The American Father" from *China Men*. Copyright © 1977, 1978, 1979, 1980 by Maxine Hong Kingston. Reprinted with the permission of Alfred A. Knopf, a division of Random House, Inc. • Rudyard Kipling, excerpt from "In San Francisco" from *American Notes: Rudyard Kipling's West* (Norman, Okla.: University of Oklahoma Press, 1981). • Jack London, excerpt from "The Story of an Eye-Witness," from *Collier's* (5 May 1906): 22. • Armistead Maupin, excerpt from *Tales of the City*. Copyright © 1978 by The Chronicle Publishing Company. Reprinted with the permission of HarperCollins Publishing, Inc. • Frank Norris, excerpt from *McTeague: A Story of San Francisco* (New York:

ILLUSTRATIONS

Scene from the Desolation: San Francisco
Museum of Modern Art, 1995. Sandow Birk.